EMMANUEL JOSEPH

The Algorithmic Atlas, Mapping How Billionaires Redraw Countries with Tech and Crypto

Copyright © 2025 by Emmanuel Joseph

All rights reserved. No part of this publication may be reproduced, stored or transmitted in any form or by any means, electronic, mechanical, photocopying, recording, scanning, or otherwise without written permission from the publisher. It is illegal to copy this book, post it to a website, or distribute it by any other means without permission.

First edition

This book was professionally typeset on Reedsy. Find out more at reedsy.com

Contents

1. Chapter 1: The Dawn of Digital Empires — 1
2. Chapter 2: The Crypto Revolution — 3
3. Chapter 3: The Rise of Digital Sovereignty — 5
4. Chapter 4: Smart Cities and Tech-Driven Utopias — 7
5. Chapter 5: The Blockchain Borders — 9
6. Chapter 6: The Influence of Tech Oligarchs — 11
7. Chapter 7: The Crypto-Colonialism — 13
8. Chapter 8: The Data Economy — 15
9. Chapter 9: The Green Tech Movement — 17
10. Chapter 10: The Tech Philanthropy Paradox — 19
11. Chapter 11: The Education Evolution — 21
12. Chapter 12: The Future of Work — 23
13. Chapter 13: The Digital Health Revolution — 25
14. Chapter 14: The Ethical Algorithm — 27
15. Chapter 15: The Cybersecurity Challenge — 29
16. Chapter 16: The Role of AI in Governance — 31
17. Chapter 17: The Global Impact of Tech and Crypto — 33

1

Chapter 1: The Dawn of Digital Empires

In the early 21st century, technology emerged not just as a tool, but as a transformative force that began to reshape societies and economies. The dawn of digital empires saw the rise of tech moguls who harnessed the power of algorithms to influence nearly every aspect of human life. From the way we communicate to the way we consume, the influence of technology grew exponentially. Billionaires in the tech industry, like digital titans, began to wield influence that rivaled traditional nation-states. Their reach extended across borders, and their innovations started to redraw the map of global power.

These tech magnates didn't just create companies; they created ecosystems. Platforms like social media, e-commerce, and cloud computing became integral to the fabric of daily life. With vast amounts of data at their disposal, these companies could predict consumer behavior, shape political opinions, and even manipulate market dynamics. The algorithms they developed became the new currency of power, and those who controlled them were akin to modern-day monarchs. As technology became more ingrained in society, the boundaries between the physical and digital worlds began to blur.

The influence of these digital empires was not confined to the virtual realm. Tech billionaires started to make significant investments in physical infrastructure, from satellite networks to smart cities. They recognized that controlling both digital and physical spaces would give them unparalleled leverage. This dual dominance allowed them to shape the future in ways previously unimaginable. As they amassed wealth and power, questions arose about their accountability and the ethical implications of their actions.

The dawn of digital empires marked the beginning of a new era where technology and wealth were inextricably linked. It was a time of great promise and great peril, as the world grappled with the implications of living in an increasingly interconnected and algorithm-driven society. The stage was set for a profound transformation, one that would challenge the very notions of sovereignty, governance, and identity.

2

Chapter 2: The Crypto Revolution

While technology giants were reshaping the digital and physical landscapes, a new revolution was brewing in the world of finance. The advent of cryptocurrencies promised to disrupt traditional financial systems and democratize access to wealth. Bitcoin, the first cryptocurrency, emerged as a decentralized digital currency that operated without the need for a central authority. Its underlying technology, blockchain, provided a transparent and secure way to record transactions. This innovation captured the imagination of millions and paved the way for the crypto revolution.

As cryptocurrencies gained traction, tech billionaires recognized their potential to create new financial paradigms. They invested heavily in blockchain technology and developed their own digital currencies. These new forms of money were not tied to any single nation, allowing for seamless cross-border transactions and challenging the dominance of traditional banks. The rise of decentralized finance (DeFi) platforms further disrupted the financial landscape, offering services like lending, borrowing, and trading without intermediaries.

The crypto revolution extended beyond finance, influencing governance and societal structures. Decentralized autonomous organizations (DAOs) emerged, allowing communities to govern themselves through smart contracts. This new form of governance promised to be more transparent and democratic, as decisions were made collectively and recorded on the blockchain. Tech billionaires supported these initiatives, seeing them as a way to decentralize power and foster innovation.

However, the crypto revolution also faced significant challenges. Regulatory bodies around the world grappled with how to oversee these new technologies, and concerns about security, fraud, and environmental impact persisted. Despite these hurdles, the momentum of the crypto revolution continued to grow, fueled by the vision of a more open and inclusive financial system. As tech billionaires pushed the boundaries of what was possible, the world watched with anticipation, wondering how this new frontier would shape the future.

3

Chapter 3: The Rise of Digital Sovereignty

As tech billionaires amassed influence through their control of digital and crypto technologies, a new concept began to take shape: digital sovereignty. This idea posited that individuals and communities could reclaim control over their digital identities and data. With the proliferation of data breaches and privacy concerns, the need for digital sovereignty became increasingly urgent. Tech billionaires, recognizing both the ethical and economic implications, began to champion this cause, developing technologies that empowered users to manage their own data.

Digital sovereignty was not just about privacy; it was about autonomy. By giving individuals control over their digital lives, tech billionaires sought to create a more equitable digital ecosystem. Decentralized technologies, such as blockchain and distributed storage, played a crucial role in this vision. These technologies allowed users to store their data securely and share it selectively, reducing the power of centralized entities like tech giants and governments.

The rise of digital sovereignty also had profound implications for nation-states. As individuals and communities asserted their digital rights, traditional notions of citizenship and governance were challenged. Virtual nations and digital communities emerged, offering new forms of belonging and identity. These virtual entities operated across borders, creating a global network of interconnected individuals who shared common values and goals. Tech billionaires supported these movements, seeing them as a way to promote innovation and disrupt outdated systems.

However, the journey towards digital sovereignty was fraught with challenges. Ensuring the security and reliability of decentralized technologies was a constant battle, and questions about the ethical use of data persisted. Despite these obstacles, the movement continued to gain traction, driven by the belief that a more just and equitable digital world was possible. The rise of digital sovereignty marked a turning point in the relationship between individuals, technology, and power, reshaping the landscape of the digital age.

4

Chapter 4: Smart Cities and Tech-Driven Utopias

Tech billionaires' vision of the future extended beyond digital sovereignty to the very cities in which we live. The concept of smart cities promised to revolutionize urban life by integrating technology into every aspect of city management. These tech-driven utopias aimed to improve efficiency, sustainability, and quality of life through the use of data and automation. From smart traffic systems to energy-efficient buildings, these innovations sought to address the challenges of urbanization in a rapidly changing world.

Smart cities were designed to be highly connected, with sensors and devices collecting data on everything from air quality to traffic flow. This data was analyzed in real-time, allowing city managers to make informed decisions and respond to issues proactively. Tech billionaires invested heavily in these initiatives, recognizing the potential to create more livable and sustainable urban environments. They collaborated with governments and urban planners to develop smart city projects around the world, from Silicon Valley to Shenzhen.

One of the key features of smart cities was their focus on sustainability. By optimizing resource usage and reducing waste, these cities aimed to minimize their environmental impact. Renewable energy sources, such as solar and wind, were integrated into the urban infrastructure, and green spaces were prioritized to improve air quality and provide recreational opportunities. Tech billionaires saw these initiatives as a way to address the pressing issue of climate change while also enhancing the quality of life for city dwellers.

Despite the promise of smart cities, there were significant challenges to overcome. Privacy concerns loomed large, as the extensive data collection required for these projects raised questions about surveillance and data security. Additionally, the implementation of smart city technologies required significant investment and infrastructure upgrades, which were not always feasible for all cities. Nonetheless, the vision of tech-driven utopias continued to inspire innovation and investment, as tech billionaires sought to create a better future for urban populations.

5

Chapter 5: The Blockchain Borders

As the influence of tech billionaires grew, they began to explore the potential of blockchain technology to redefine borders and governance. Blockchain, with its decentralized and transparent nature, offered a new way to manage and verify transactions, records, and identities. This technology had the potential to create a new form of borderless governance, where individuals could participate in decentralized systems that operated independently of traditional nation-states. Tech billionaires saw this as an opportunity to promote innovation and challenge the status quo.

One of the key applications of blockchain in this context was the creation of digital identities. These identities were secure, tamper-proof, and portable, allowing individuals to prove their identity and access services across borders. This was particularly impactful for marginalized populations, such as refugees and stateless individuals, who often faced barriers to accessing essential services. Tech billionaires invested in projects that aimed to provide digital identities to these populations, empowering them to participate in the global economy.

Blockchain also enabled the creation of decentralized autonomous organizations (DAOs), which allowed communities to govern themselves without the need for a central authority. These organizations operated on smart contracts, which automatically executed agreements based on predefined conditions. This new form of governance promised to be more transparent, democratic, and efficient. Tech billionaires supported these initiatives, seeing them as a way to decentralize power and foster innovation.

However, the implementation of blockchain borders was not without challenges. Ensuring the security and scalability of these systems was a constant battle, and questions about the ethical use of data persisted. Despite these obstacles, the vision of blockchain borders continued to inspire innovation and investment, as tech billionaires sought to create a more just and equitable global society.

6

Chapter 6: The Influence of Tech Oligarchs

As tech billionaires amassed unprecedented wealth and influence, they began to shape not just the digital world, but the political landscape as well. These tech oligarchs used their resources to fund political campaigns, lobby for favorable regulations, and promote policies that aligned with their interests. Their influence extended across borders, as they supported political movements and candidates around the world. This new form of political power challenged traditional notions of governance and raised questions about accountability and democracy.

Tech oligarchs also leveraged their platforms to shape public opinion. Social media, search engines, and other digital platforms became powerful tools for influencing political discourse. By controlling the flow of information, these tech moguls could sway public opinion and shape the outcomes of elections. This raised concerns about the concentration of power in the hands of a few individuals and the potential for manipulation and misinformation.

Despite these concerns, tech oligarchs also used their influence for positive change. Many invested in philanthropic initiatives that aimed to address global challenges such as poverty, education, and climate change. They supported projects that promoted innovation and economic development, often focusing on marginalized populations. These efforts demonstrated the potential for tech billionaires to use their resources for the greater good, even as their influence raised questions about the balance of power in society.

The influence of tech oligarchs marked a significant shift in the dynamics of political power. As they continued to shape the digital and political landscapes, the world grappled with the implications of living in an increasingly interconnected and algorithm-driven society. The stage was set for a profound transformation, one that would challenge the very notions of sovereignty, governance, and identity.

7

Chapter 7: The Crypto-Colonialism

The rise of cryptocurrencies and blockchain technology also gave rise to a new form of economic imperialism: crypto-colonialism. Tech billionaires, with their vast resources and technological expertise, began to invest heavily in developing countries, bringing digital infrastructure and financial services to underserved populations. While these initiatives promised to promote economic development and financial inclusion, they also raised concerns about exploitation and dependency.

Crypto-colonialism involved the creation of digital economies that operated independently of traditional financial systems. Tech billionaires introduced cryptocurrencies and blockchain-based financial services to these regions, providing access to banking, lending, and investment opportunities. This allowed individuals and businesses to participate in the global economy, often for the first time. However, it also created new dependencies, as these digital economies relied heavily on the infrastructure and platforms controlled by tech giants.

The impact of crypto-colonialism extended beyond finance. Tech billionaires also invested in digital education, healthcare, and governance initiatives, aiming to improve the quality of life in developing countries. While these efforts brought significant benefits, they also raised questions about cultural imperialism and the erosion of local traditions and practices. The imposition of digital technologies on these societies often came at the expense of local autonomy and control.

Despite these challenges, crypto-colonialism continued to gain traction, driven by the vision of a more connected and inclusive global society. As tech billionaires pushed the boundaries of what was possible, the world watched with anticipation, wondering how this new frontier would shape the future. The rise of crypto-colonialism marked a turning point in the relationship between technology, wealth, and power, reshaping the landscape of the digital age.

8

Chapter 8: The Data Economy

As technology continued to evolve, data emerged as the new oil of the digital age. Tech billionaires recognized the immense value of data and began to amass vast quantities of it. From social media interactions to online shopping habits, every digital interaction generated data that could be analyzed and monetized. This data economy became the backbone of the digital empires, driving innovation and shaping the future of commerce, entertainment, and even governance.

The data economy was built on the premise that data could be used to predict and influence human behavior. By analyzing patterns and trends, tech companies could develop personalized products and services that catered to individual preferences. This allowed them to optimize their operations, increase efficiency, and maximize profits. Tech billionaires invested heavily in artificial intelligence and machine learning technologies that could process and analyze vast amounts of data, unlocking new insights and opportunities.

However, the rise of the data economy also raised significant ethical and privacy concerns. The extensive collection and analysis of personal data often occurred without individuals' explicit consent, leading to concerns about surveillance and data breaches. Tech billionaires faced increasing scrutiny from regulators and the public, who called for greater transparency and accountability in the handling of data.

Despite these challenges, the data economy continued to thrive, driven by the belief that data was the key to unlocking new frontiers of innovation and economic growth. Tech billionaires played a central role in this transformation, using their resources and expertise to shape the future of the digital age. As the world grappled with the implications of living in a data-driven society, the influence of tech billionaires showed no signs of waning.

9

Chapter 9: The Green Tech Movement

Amid growing concerns about climate change and environmental degradation, tech billionaires began to turn their attention to sustainability. The green tech movement aimed to leverage technology to address environmental challenges and promote sustainable development. This movement was driven by the belief that technology could provide innovative solutions to reduce carbon emissions, conserve resources, and protect natural ecosystems. Tech billionaires invested heavily in renewable energy, clean transportation, and green building technologies, seeking to create a more sustainable future.

One of the key areas of focus for the green tech movement was renewable energy. Tech billionaires funded the development of solar, wind, and hydroelectric power, aiming to reduce reliance on fossil fuels and mitigate the impacts of climate change. These investments led to significant advancements in renewable energy technologies, making them more efficient and cost-effective. Smart grids and energy storage solutions were also developed to optimize the distribution and use of renewable energy, further enhancing sustainability.

Clean transportation was another priority for the green tech movement. Electric vehicles (EVs) and autonomous transportation systems were developed to reduce greenhouse gas emissions and improve urban mobility. Tech billionaires supported the expansion of EV charging infrastructure and invested in research and development to improve battery technology and vehicle performance. These efforts aimed to create a more sustainable and efficient transportation system, reducing the environmental impact of commuting and travel.

Green building technologies were also a focus of the green tech movement. Tech billionaires funded the development of energy-efficient building materials and construction methods, aiming to reduce the carbon footprint of the built environment. Smart buildings equipped with sensors and automation systems were designed to optimize energy use and enhance occupant comfort. These innovations promised to create healthier, more sustainable living and working spaces, contributing to the overall goals of the green tech movement.

10

Chapter 10: The Tech Philanthropy Paradox

While tech billionaires amassed immense wealth and influence, they also faced growing scrutiny and criticism. In response, many turned to philanthropy as a way to give back to society and address global challenges. Tech philanthropy, however, presented a paradox: while it aimed to promote positive change, it also raised questions about accountability, transparency, and the concentration of power in the hands of a few individuals. This paradox became a defining feature of the relationship between tech billionaires and society.

Tech philanthropists focused on a wide range of issues, from education and healthcare to poverty alleviation and environmental conservation. They funded initiatives that aimed to provide access to quality education, improve healthcare outcomes, and promote economic development in underserved communities. These efforts demonstrated the potential for tech billionaires to use their resources for the greater good, leveraging their wealth and expertise to drive meaningful change.

However, the concentration of philanthropic power in the hands of a few tech magnates also raised concerns. Critics argued that tech philanthropy often lacked transparency and accountability, as decisions about how to allocate resources were made by a small group of individuals rather than democratic institutions. This concentration of power also led to concerns about the potential for philanthropy to be used as a tool for personal or corporate gain, rather than a genuine effort to promote social good.

Despite these challenges, tech philanthropy continued to play a significant role in addressing global challenges. Tech billionaires used their resources and influence to support innovative solutions and drive progress on critical issues. As the world grappled with the implications of living in an increasingly interconnected and algorithm-driven society, the paradox of tech philanthropy highlighted the complex relationship between wealth, power, and social responsibility.

11

Chapter 11: The Education Evolution

The digital revolution brought about significant changes in the field of education. Tech billionaires recognized the potential of technology to transform the way we learn and teach, and they invested heavily in edtech (educational technology) initiatives. The goal was to create more accessible, personalized, and effective learning experiences that could address the diverse needs of students around the world. The education evolution was driven by the belief that technology could democratize access to knowledge and empower individuals to reach their full potential.

One of the key innovations in edtech was the development of online learning platforms. These platforms provided students with access to a wide range of courses and educational resources, allowing them to learn at their own pace and on their own schedule. Tech billionaires funded the creation of massive open online courses (MOOCs), which offered high-quality education from top universities to anyone with an internet connection. This democratization of education had the potential to break down barriers and create new opportunities for lifelong learning.

Personalized learning was another focus of the education evolution. Tech billionaires invested in artificial intelligence and data analytics to develop adaptive learning systems that tailored instruction to the individual needs of each student. These systems used data on student performance to identify strengths and weaknesses, providing targeted feedback and personalized learning pathways. The goal was to create more effective and engaging learning experiences that could improve student outcomes and reduce achievement gaps.

The education evolution also extended to the classroom. Tech billionaires funded the development of digital tools and resources that enhanced traditional teaching methods. Interactive whiteboards, virtual reality (VR) simulations, and gamified learning experiences were introduced to make learning more interactive and immersive. Teachers were provided with professional development opportunities to integrate technology into their instruction, enhancing their ability to support student learning.

Despite the promise of edtech, there were significant challenges to overcome. Ensuring equitable access to technology and addressing the digital divide were critical issues, as not all students had the same access to devices and internet connectivity. Additionally, concerns about data privacy and the ethical use of student data persisted. Nonetheless, the education evolution continued to drive innovation and investment, as tech billionaires sought to create a more inclusive and effective education system for all.

12

Chapter 12: The Future of Work

The rise of technology and automation brought about profound changes in the world of work. Tech billionaires recognized the potential of these innovations to increase productivity and efficiency, but they also understood the challenges they posed for workers and the labor market. The future of work was shaped by the interplay between technological advancements and the need to create meaningful employment opportunities in a rapidly changing economy.

One of the key trends in the future of work was the rise of remote and flexible work arrangements. The COVID-19 pandemic accelerated the adoption of remote work, as companies and workers adapted to new ways of working. Tech billionaires invested in digital collaboration tools and platforms that enabled remote work, making it possible for employees to work from anywhere in the world. This shift had the potential to increase work-life balance and provide greater flexibility for workers, but it also raised questions about productivity, accountability, and the erosion of traditional office culture.

Automation and artificial intelligence were also transforming the labor market. Tech billionaires funded the development of AI-powered systems that could perform tasks previously done by humans, from manufacturing and logistics to customer service and data analysis. While these technologies had the potential to increase efficiency and reduce costs, they also posed significant challenges for workers whose jobs were at risk of being automated. Tech billionaires supported initiatives to reskill and upskill workers, providing them with the training and education needed to thrive in the new economy.

The gig economy was another feature of the future of work. Tech billionaires developed platforms that connected workers with short-term, flexible employment opportunities, from ride-sharing and delivery services to freelance and contract work. While the gig economy provided new opportunities for income and entrepreneurship, it also raised concerns about job security, benefits, and workers' rights. Tech billionaires faced increasing scrutiny from regulators and the public, who called for greater protections and support for gig workers.

Despite these challenges, the future of work continued to evolve, driven by the vision of a more flexible, efficient, and inclusive labor market. Tech billionaires played a central role in this transformation, using their resources and expertise to shape the future of work in the digital age. As the world grappled with the implications of living in an increasingly interconnected and algorithm-driven society, the future of work remained a critical area of focus and innovation.

13

Chapter 13: The Digital Health Revolution

The integration of technology into healthcare brought about a digital health revolution that promised to transform the way we approach wellness and medical care. Tech billionaires recognized the potential of digital health technologies to improve patient outcomes, reduce costs, and increase access to care. They invested heavily in innovations such as telemedicine, wearable devices, and artificial intelligence, driving a new era of healthcare that was more personalized, efficient, and accessible.

Telemedicine emerged as a key innovation in the digital health revolution. Tech billionaires funded the development of platforms that allowed patients to consult with healthcare providers remotely, using video conferencing and secure messaging. This technology made it possible for individuals to access medical care from the comfort of their homes, reducing the need for in-person visits and increasing convenience. Telemedicine also expanded access to healthcare in underserved and remote areas, where medical resources were often limited.

Wearable devices and health monitoring technologies played a significant role in the digital health revolution. Tech billionaires supported the creation of devices that could track vital signs, physical activity, and other health metrics in real time. These devices provided valuable data that could be used to monitor chronic conditions, detect early signs of illness, and promote healthy lifestyles. The integration of wearable devices with mobile apps and cloud platforms allowed for continuous monitoring and personalized health recommendations, empowering individuals to take control of their health.

Artificial intelligence was another critical component of the digital health revolution. Tech billionaires invested in AI-powered systems that could analyze medical data, assist in diagnosis, and develop personalized treatment plans. These systems used machine learning algorithms to process vast amounts of data, identifying patterns and trends that could inform medical decision-making. AI also played a role in drug discovery and development, accelerating the research process and increasing the likelihood of finding effective treatments.

Despite the promise of digital health technologies, there were significant challenges to overcome. Ensuring the privacy and security of medical data was a top priority, as data breaches and cyberattacks posed serious risks to patient confidentiality. Additionally, the adoption of digital health technologies required significant investment in infrastructure and training, which could be a barrier for some healthcare providers. Nonetheless, the digital health revolution continued to drive innovation and investment, as tech billionaires sought to create a more effective and equitable healthcare system.

14

Chapter 14: The Ethical Algorithm

As algorithms became increasingly integrated into our daily lives, questions about their ethical use and impact on society came to the forefront. Tech billionaires, who wielded significant influence through their control of these algorithms, faced growing pressure to address the ethical implications of their creations. The ethical algorithm movement aimed to ensure that algorithms were designed and implemented in ways that promoted fairness, transparency, and accountability.

One of the key concerns in the ethical algorithm movement was bias. Algorithms, which were often trained on historical data, could inadvertently perpetuate existing biases and inequalities. Tech billionaires funded research and development efforts to create more equitable algorithms that minimized bias and promoted fairness. This involved developing techniques for detecting and mitigating bias in data, as well as creating diverse and representative datasets that better reflected the complexities of the real world.

Transparency was another critical issue in the ethical algorithm movement. Tech billionaires supported initiatives to make algorithms more transparent and understandable to the public. This included developing tools and frameworks for explaining how algorithms made decisions, as well as creating standards for auditing and evaluating algorithmic systems. The goal was to build trust and confidence in the use of algorithms, ensuring that they operated in ways that were consistent with societal values and expectations.

Accountability was also a key focus of the ethical algorithm movement. Tech billionaires advocated for the creation of regulatory frameworks and oversight mechanisms to ensure that algorithms were used responsibly. This involved establishing guidelines for the ethical use of algorithms, as well as creating mechanisms for addressing grievances and holding organizations accountable for algorithmic decisions. The goal was to create a balanced approach that promoted innovation while protecting individual rights and societal interests.

The ethical algorithm movement highlighted the need for a more thoughtful and responsible approach to the development and use of algorithms. As tech billionaires continued to shape the digital landscape, they recognized the importance of addressing the ethical implications of their creations. The movement aimed to ensure that algorithms were used in ways that promoted fairness, transparency, and accountability, creating a more just and equitable digital society.

15

Chapter 15: The Cybersecurity Challenge

The increasing reliance on digital technologies brought about significant cybersecurity challenges. As tech billionaires developed and implemented new technologies, they faced the constant threat of cyberattacks and data breaches. The cybersecurity challenge required a proactive and collaborative approach to protect digital infrastructure, data, and privacy. Tech billionaires invested heavily in cybersecurity research and development, aiming to create more secure and resilient systems that could withstand evolving threats.

One of the key areas of focus in the cybersecurity challenge was protecting critical infrastructure. Tech billionaires funded initiatives to secure essential services such as power grids, transportation systems, and communication networks. This involved developing advanced threat detection and response systems, as well as creating more robust encryption and authentication methods. The goal was to ensure the continuity and reliability of critical infrastructure, even in the face of sophisticated cyberattacks.

Data privacy was another critical concern in the cybersecurity challenge. Tech billionaires supported efforts to create more secure data storage and transmission methods, protecting sensitive information from unauthorized access and breaches. This included developing encryption technologies, secure communication protocols, and privacy-preserving data analytics techniques. The goal was to strike a balance between the need for data-driven innovation and the protection of individual privacy.

Collaboration was essential to addressing the cybersecurity challenge. Tech billionaires recognized the importance of working together with governments, industry partners, and academic institutions to share knowledge and resources. This included participating in information-sharing initiatives, supporting cybersecurity education and training programs, and contributing to the development of global cybersecurity standards. The goal was to create a united front against cyber threats, leveraging collective expertise and resources to enhance digital security.

Despite these efforts, the cybersecurity challenge remained a constant and evolving threat. Tech billionaires continued to invest in innovative solutions and best practices to stay ahead of cybercriminals and protect the digital infrastructure. The cybersecurity challenge underscored the importance of vigilance, collaboration, and continuous improvement in the face of an increasingly interconnected and digitized world.

16

Chapter 16: The Role of AI in Governance

As artificial intelligence (AI) became more advanced, its potential to transform governance and public administration became increasingly apparent. Tech billionaires recognized the potential of AI to improve the efficiency and effectiveness of government services, enhance decision-making, and promote transparency. The role of AI in governance aimed to leverage technology to create more responsive, data-driven, and accountable public institutions.

One of the key applications of AI in governance was in public service delivery. Tech billionaires funded the development of AI-powered systems that could streamline processes, automate routine tasks, and provide personalized services to citizens. This included applications such as chatbots for customer service, predictive analytics for resource allocation, and AI-driven decision support systems for policymakers. The goal was to enhance the quality and accessibility of public services, making them more efficient and user-centric.

AI also played a significant role in enhancing transparency and accountability in governance. Tech billionaires supported initiatives to create AI-driven systems for monitoring and auditing government activities. These systems could analyze vast amounts of data to detect patterns of corruption, inefficiency, and malpractice. By providing real-time insights and recommendations, AI systems helped to promote greater transparency and accountability in public administration, fostering trust between citizens and government institutions.

Data-driven decision-making was another critical application of AI in governance. Tech billionaires invested in AI technologies that could analyze large datasets to inform policy decisions and optimize resource allocation. This included applications such as predictive modeling for public health, transportation planning, and disaster response. By leveraging AI, governments could make more informed and evidence-based decisions, improving outcomes and addressing complex challenges more effectively.

Despite the promise of AI in governance, there were significant challenges to overcome. Ensuring the ethical use of AI, protecting individual privacy, and addressing biases in AI systems were critical concerns. Tech billionaires recognized the importance of developing guidelines and frameworks for the responsible use of AI in governance. The role of AI in governance highlighted the potential for technology to enhance public administration while also underscoring the need for thoughtful and ethical implementation.

17

Chapter 17: The Global Impact of Tech and Crypto

The influence of tech billionaires extended far beyond the digital and financial realms, shaping the global landscape in profound and often unexpected ways. The global impact of tech and crypto was felt across economies, societies, and cultures, as the innovations and investments of tech billionaires redefined the boundaries of what was possible. This chapter explores the far-reaching effects of tech and crypto on the world, highlighting the opportunities and challenges that lie ahead.

One of the most significant impacts of tech and crypto was on the global economy. Tech billionaires' investments in digital infrastructure, financial technologies, and renewable energy drove economic growth and innovation. These investments created new industries, jobs, and opportunities, contributing to the overall prosperity of nations. However, the concentration of wealth and power in the hands of a few tech magnates also raised concerns about inequality and the equitable distribution of resources.

Tech and crypto also had a profound impact on society and culture. The proliferation of digital technologies transformed the way people communicated, learned, and interacted with one another. Social media platforms, online education, and virtual communities created new forms of social engagement and cultural expression. Tech billionaires played a central role in shaping these digital ecosystems, influencing the norms and values of the digital age.

The environmental impact of tech and crypto was another critical consideration. While tech billionaires invested in green technologies and renewable energy, the digital infrastructure required for tech and crypto also had a significant carbon footprint. The energy consumption of data centers, blockchain networks, and digital devices raised concerns about sustainability and environmental responsibility. Tech billionaires faced the challenge of balancing innovation with the need to minimize environmental impact and promote sustainable practices.

The global impact of tech and crypto highlighted the interconnectedness of the modern world. The innovations and investments of tech billionaires had far-reaching effects that transcended borders, creating both opportunities and challenges for nations

The Algorithmic Atlas: Mapping How Billionaires Redraw Countries with Tech and Crypto

In a world where technology and cryptocurrency are reshaping the very fabric of society, tech billionaires are emerging as powerful forces that transcend traditional borders and institutions. "The Algorithmic Atlas" delves into this transformative era, where digital empires and blockchain innovations are redrawing the map of global influence.

From the dawn of digital empires and the rise of cryptocurrencies to the concept of digital sovereignty and the creation of smart cities, this book explores how tech magnates are leveraging their wealth and expertise to shape the future. It examines the ethical implications of their actions, the challenges of ensuring digital privacy and security, and the impact of their investments on global economies, societies, and cultures.

Through seventeen thought-provoking chapters, "The Algorithmic Atlas" provides a comprehensive overview of the ways in which technology and crypto are redefining power and governance. It highlights the potential for positive change, while also addressing the complexities and ethical dilemmas that arise in this new frontier. Join us on a journey to understand the profound impact of tech and crypto on our world, and the billionaires who are at the helm of this digital revolution.

www.ingramcontent.com/pod-product-compliance
Lightning Source LLC
LaVergne TN
LVHW020458080526
838202LV00057B/6024